Look at the

by Tammy Jones

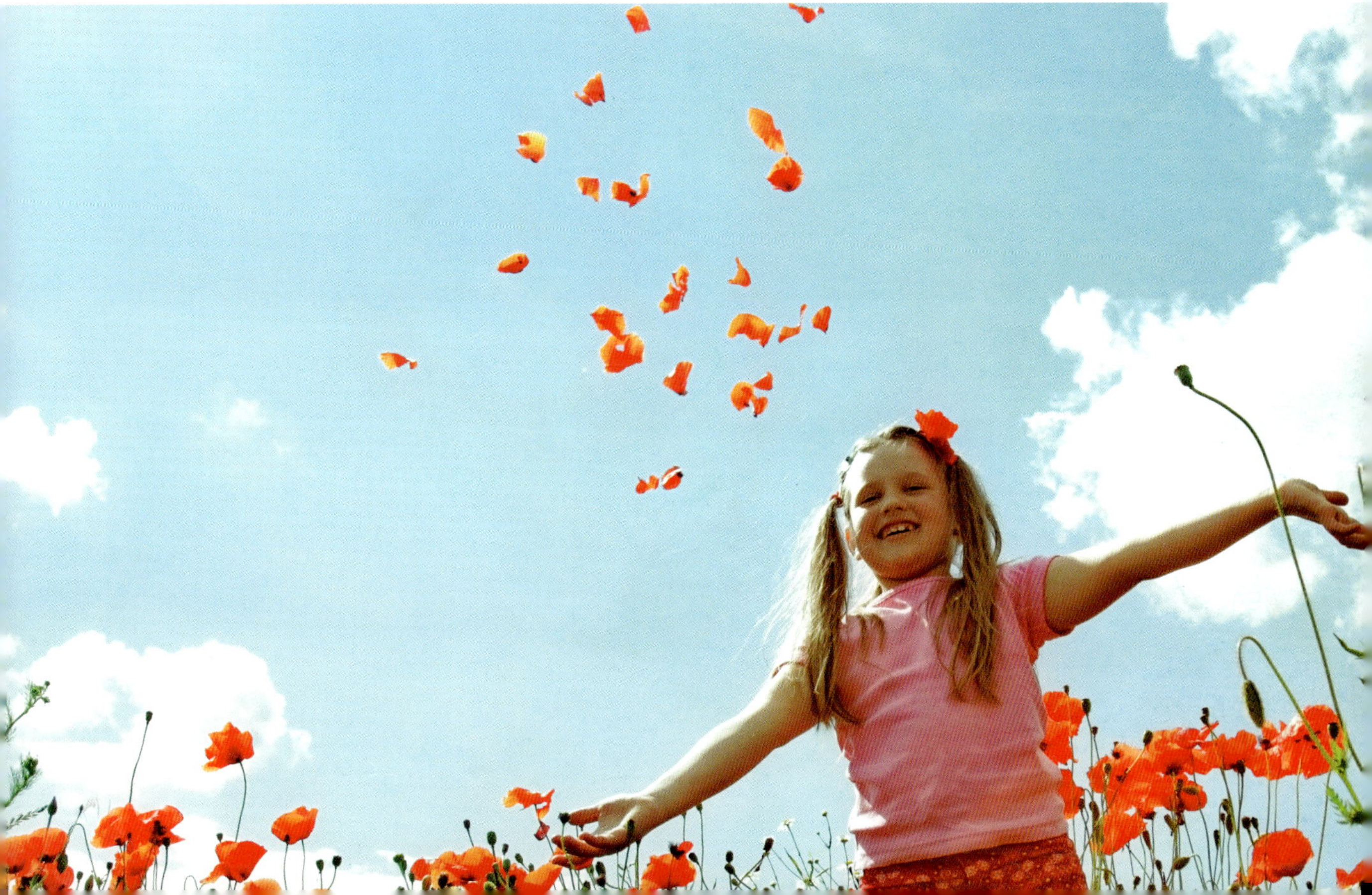

Picture Words

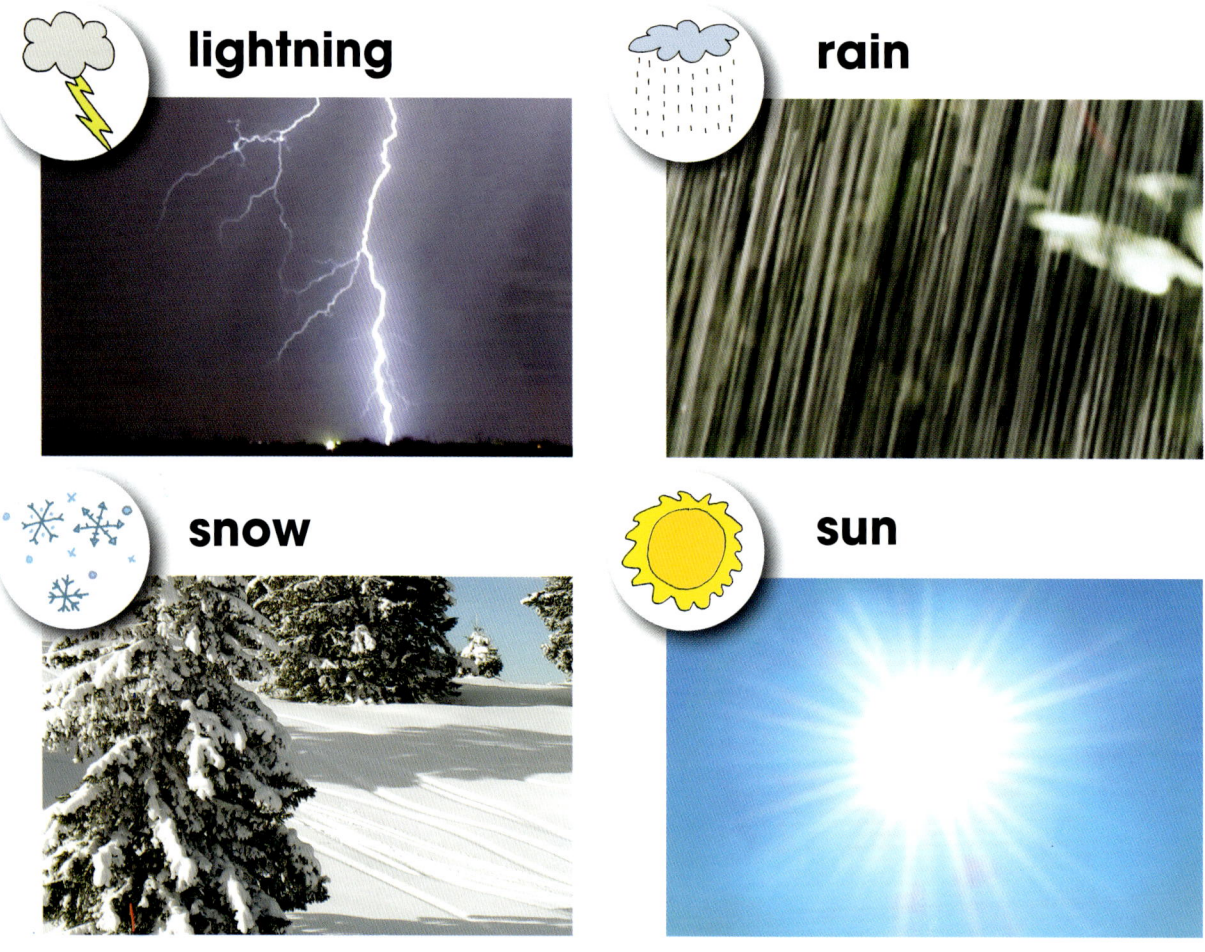

wind

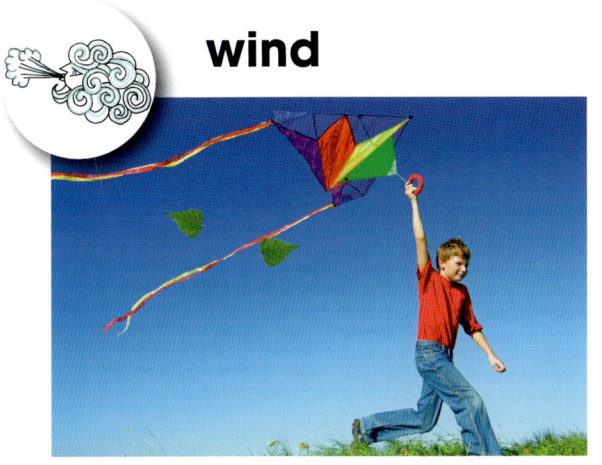

Sight Words

| can |
| I |
| see |
| the |

I can see the 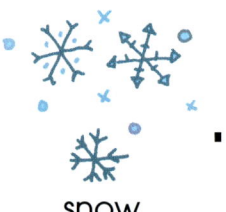.

snow

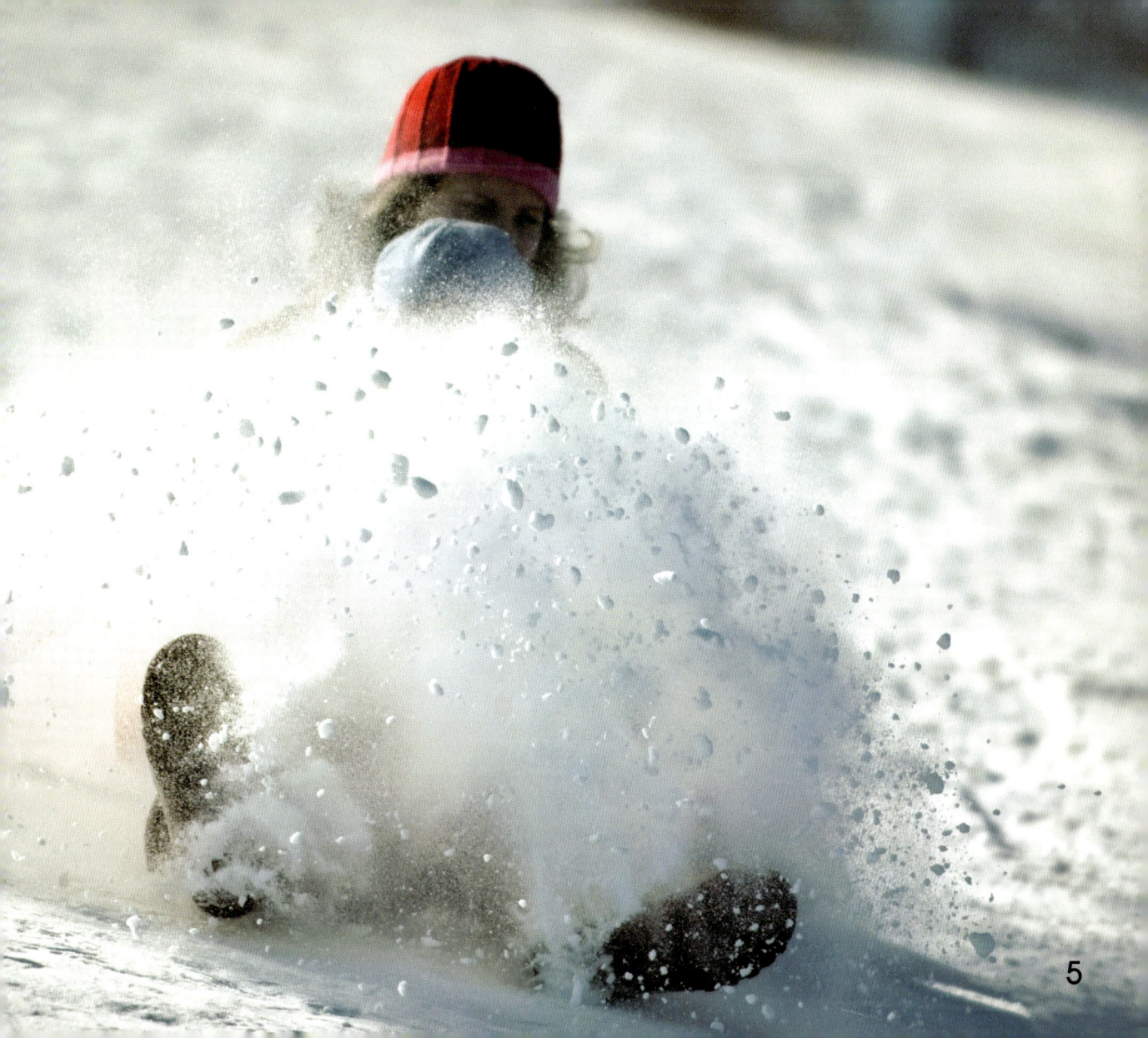

I can see the 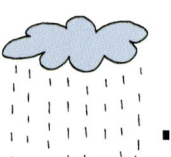.

rain

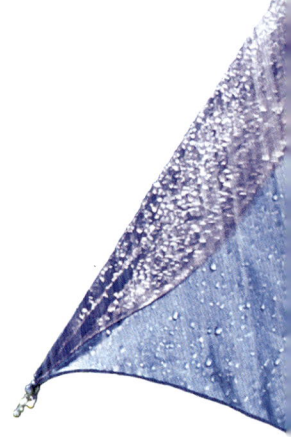

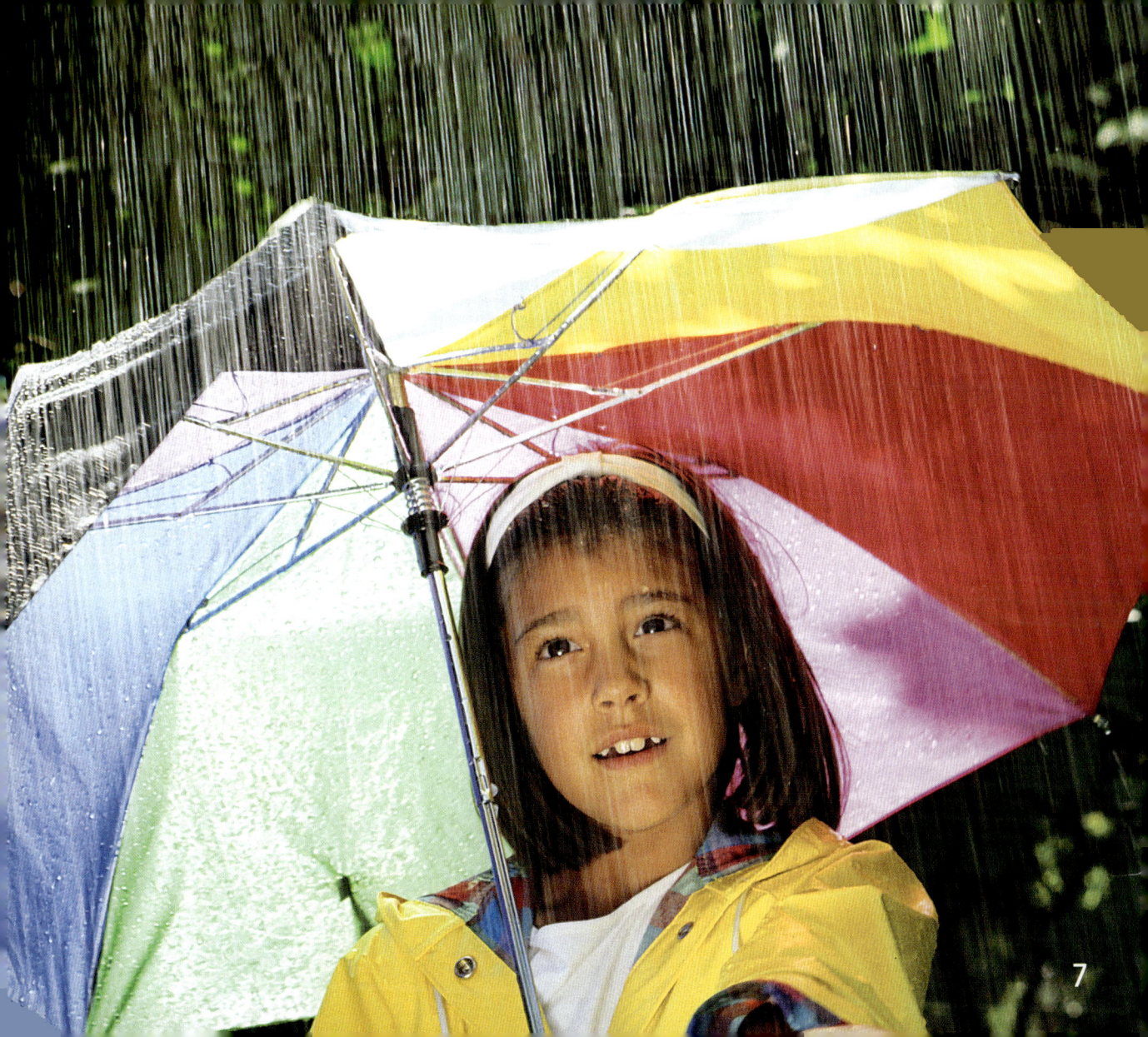

I can see the sun.

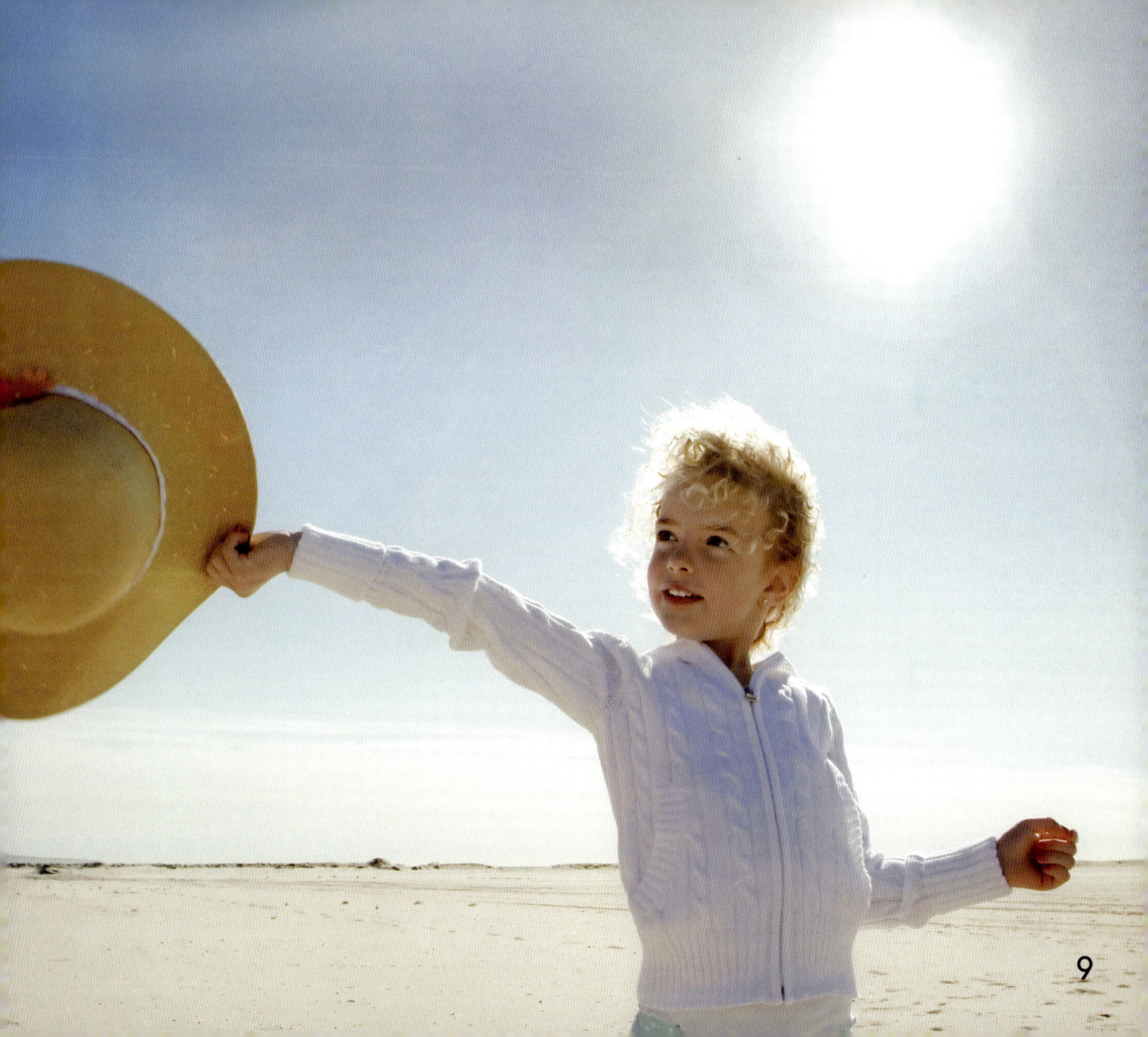

I can see the 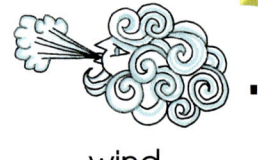.

wind

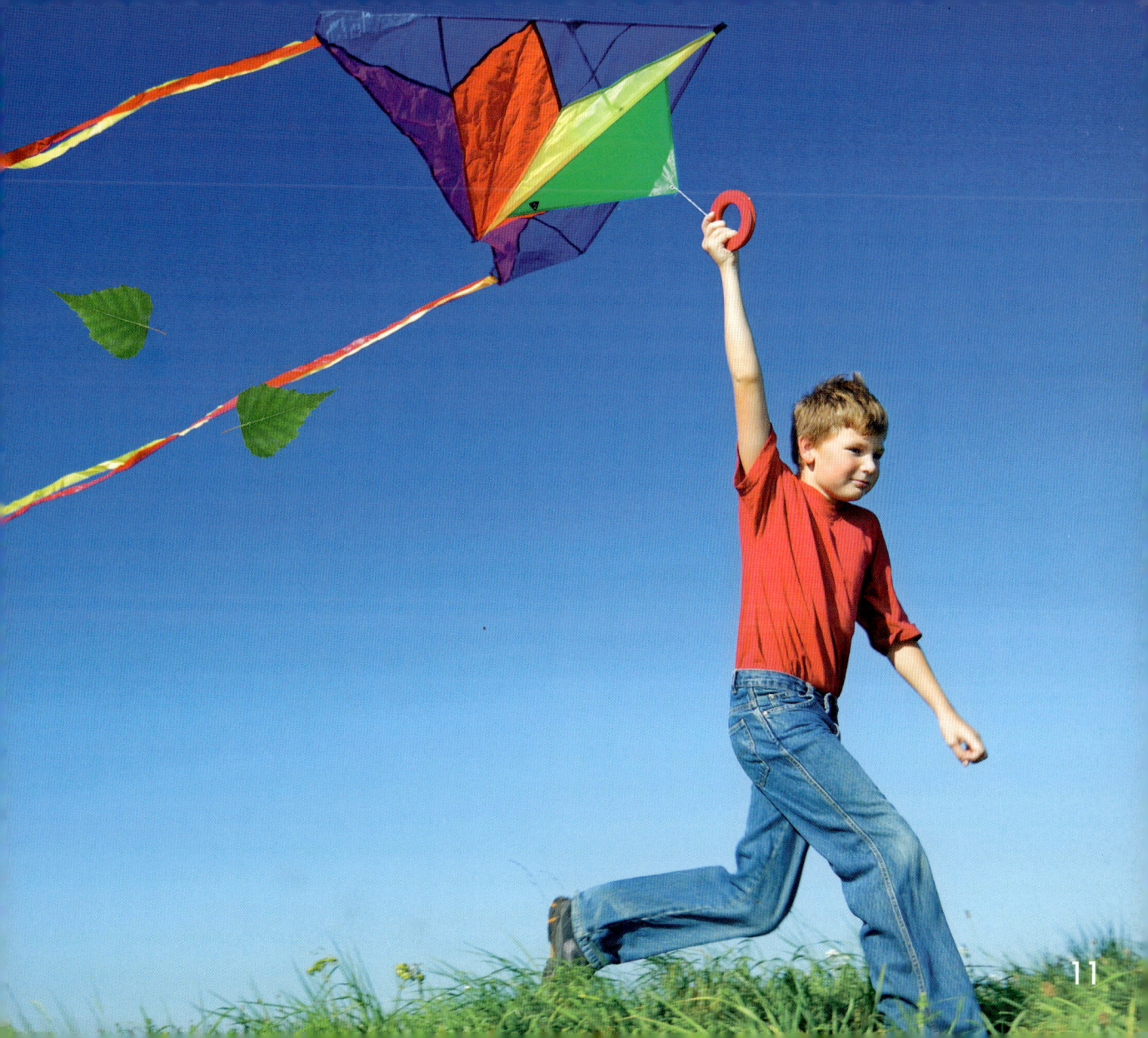

I can see the !

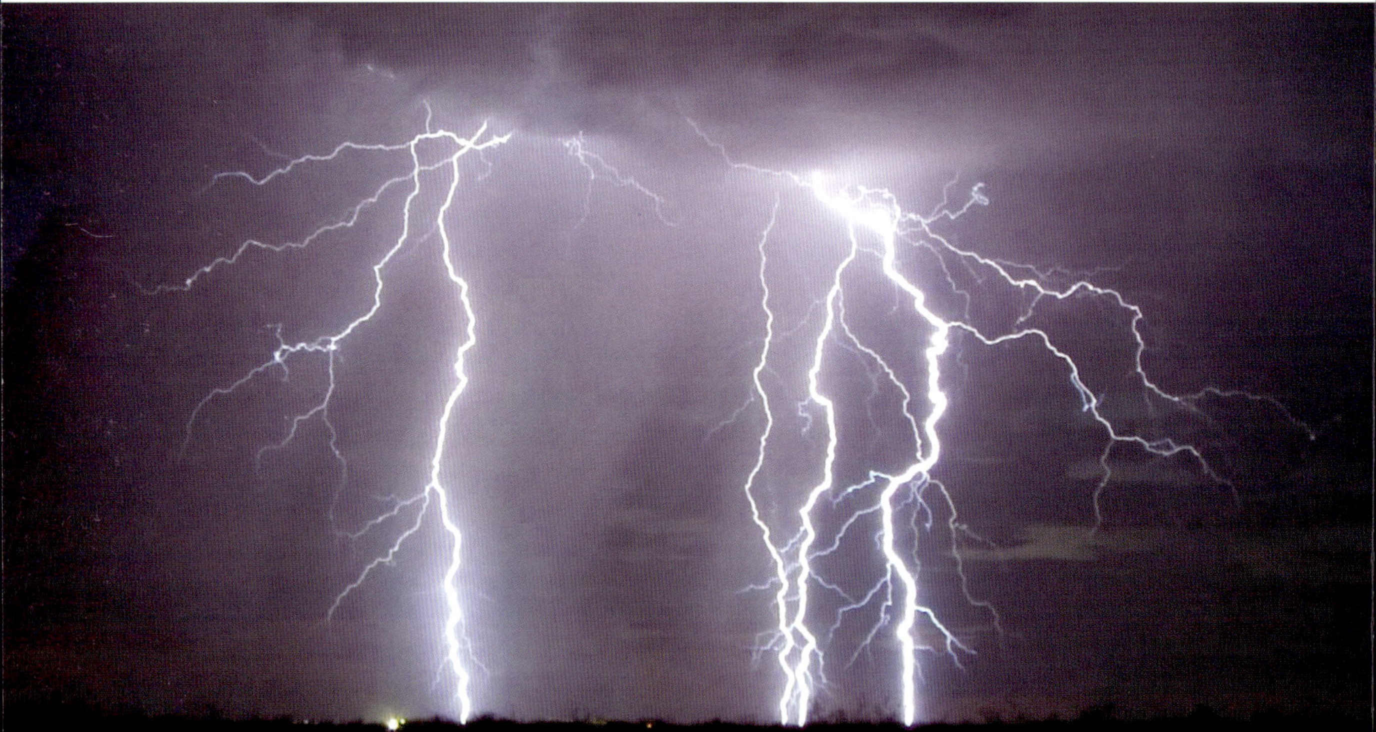